The Boer War: The History and Legacy of the Conflict that Solidified British Rule in South Africa

By Charles River Editors

A picture of Boer militia in 1900

About Charles River Editors

Charles River Editors is a boutique digital publishing company, specializing in bringing history back to life with educational and engaging books on a wide range of topics. Keep up to date with our new and free offerings with this 5 second sign up on our weekly mailing list, and visit Our Kindle Author Page to see other recently published Kindle titles.

We make these books for you and always want to know our readers' opinions, so we encourage you to leave reviews and look forward to publishing new and exciting titles each week.

Introduction

A painting of the SS *Cornwall* departing for the war

The Boer War

The Boer War: The History and Legacy of the Conflict that Solidified British Rule in South Africa looks at the controversial fighting and the manner in which it affected the 20th century. Along with pictures and a bibliography, you will learn about the Boer War like never before.

The Boer War: The History and Legacy of the Conflict that Solidified British Rule in South Africa

About Charles River Editors

Introduction

   The Origins of British Involvement in South Africa

   The Jameson Raid

   Three Sieges

   Turning the Tide

   The British Response

   The Peace

   Online Resources

   Bibliography

Free Books by Charles River Editors

Discounted Books by Charles River Editors

The Origins of British Involvement in South Africa

"The Boers were hostile toward indigenous African peoples, with whom they fought frequent range wars, and toward the government of the Cape, which was attempting to control Boer movements and commerce. They overtly compared their way of life to that of the Israel patriarchs of the Bible, developing independent patriarchal communities based upon a mobile pastoralist economy. Staunch Calvinists, they saw themselves as the children of God in the wilderness, a Christian elect divinely ordained to rule the land and the backward natives therein. By the end of the 18th century the cultural links between the Boers and their urban counterparts were diminishing, although both groups continued to speak a type of Flemish." – Encyclopaedia Britannica

The Boer War was the defining conflict of South African history and one of the most important conflicts in the history of the British Empire. Naturally, complicated geopolitics underscored it.

The European history of South Africa began with the 1652 arrival of a small Dutch flotilla in Table Bay, at the southern extremity of the African continent, which made landfall with a view to establishing a victualing station to service passing Dutch East India Company (*Vereenigde Oost-Indische Compagnie*) ships. The Dutch at that point largely dominated the East Indian Trade, and it was their establishment of the settlement of *Kaapstad*, or Cape Town, that set in motion the lengthy and often turbulent history of South Africa.

For over a century, the Cape remained a Dutch East India Company settlement, and in the interests of limiting expenses, strict parameters were established to avoid the development of a colony. As religious intolerance in Europe drove a steady trickle of outward emigration, however, Dutch settlers began to informally expand beyond the Cape, settling the sparsely inhabited hinterland to the north and east of Cape Town. In doing so, they fell increasingly outside the administrative scope of the Company, and they developed an individualistic worldview, characterized by self-dependence and self-reliance. They were also bonded as a society by a rigorous and literal interpretation of the Old Testament. In their wake, towards the end of the 17th century, followed a wave of French Huguenot immigrants, fleeing a renewal of anti-Protestantism in Europe. They were integrated over the succeeding generations, creating a hybridized language and culture that emerged in due course as the Cape Dutch, The Afrikaner or the Boer.

The Napoleonic Wars radically altered the old, established European power dynamics, and in 1795, the British, now emerging as the globe's naval superpower, assumed control of the Cape as part of the spoils of war. In doing so, they recognized the enormous strategic value of the Cape as global shipping routes were developing and expanding. Possession passed back and forth once or twice, but more or less from that point onwards, the British established their presence at the Cape, which they held until the unification of South Africa in 1910.

The effects of British rule in the Cape were profound. Under Dutch East India Company rule, a laissez-faire attitude characterized territorial government, and beyond the immediate orbit of Cape Town, the fringe settlers, or the emerging Boer society, were left largely to their own devices. The British, however, with an infinitely more comprehensive view of the colonial administration, actively extended control into the hinterland, imposing standardized systems of government and law on a people long accustomed to units of government that extended no further than the family. This was inflamed by the abolition of slavery in the early 1830s, and further still by the organized settlement of the Eastern Cape by British funded (and English-speaking) colonization.

A Boer family in the 1880s

The net result of this was a decision taken in the early 1830s by a radical fringe of Boer to leave the Cape region altogether, in an organized exodus known as The Great Trek. This carried waves of migrating Boer, known as Voortrekkers, or Forward-movers, north into the unsettled interior of the subcontinent. Beyond the Vaal River, and east into the future Natal, the migrating Boer came up against two powerful, independent native kingdoms, the Zulu and the amaNdebele. Several dramatic engagements took place that saw isolated Boer parties attacked by significant legions of disciplined native infantry, but since the Boer were armed with traditional weapons and used cannonades and musketry against their opponents' mounted assaults, these tribes were ultimately defeated. Such improbable victories as these, against such phenomenal odds, established the bedrock of Boer mythology and served to confirm to a pious people that this was indeed a land promised to them by God.

Three Boer republics were thereafter founded. These were the Orange Free State (Oranje-Vrijstaat), the Transvaal, or Zuid-Afrikaansche Republiek (ZAR), and the Republic of Natalia. The first two were landlocked, of little interest to the British, but the latter, Natal, occupied the coastal littoral east of the Drakensberg Mountains, another potentially strategic maritime location that the British could hardly allow to fall out of their control. In 1843, a naval expedition was sent to occupy Port Natal, the future Durban, and the territory was annexed and declared a British colony.

This, then, set the stage for the political evolution of the subcontinent of South Africa. The British acknowledged the existence of the Boer republics, and under certain conditions, the British even recognized their independence. Nonetheless, the British retained an unspoken option on both territories, should circumstances ever require it.

For the time being, however, the two republics had nothing much of strategic or economic interest to offer, so they were left to develop along their own preferred lines. The British, on the whole, were interested in the territory only from a naval/strategic perspective, and so long as the key ports lay in British hands, the interior could languish under Boer control indefinitely.

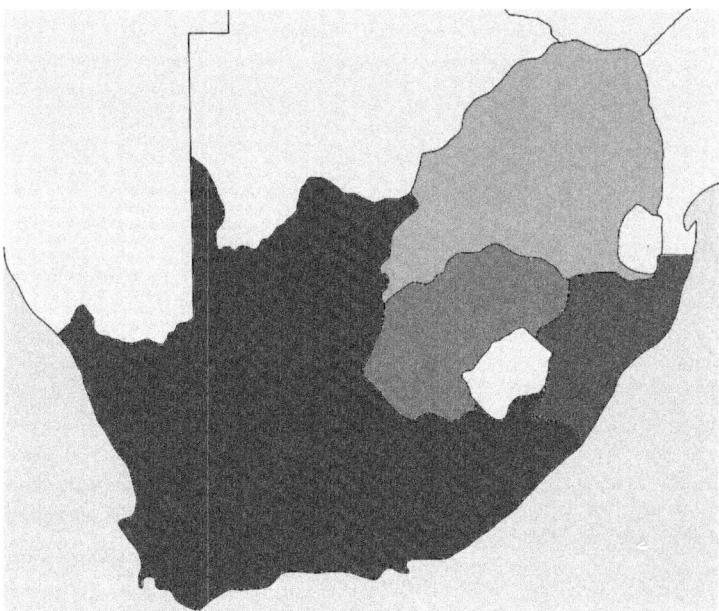

A map of the British Cape Colony (blue), Transvaal (green), the Orange Free State (orange), and the Natal (red)

This status quo might have held, but two key events took place. The first of these was the discovery of rich diamond deposits in a vaguely demarcated border region between the Cape and the Orange Free State, which inevitably altered the British view of things. That discovery was followed soon after by the discovery of what were then the richest gold fields in the world, located in the heartland of the Transvaal. Almost overnight, South Africa became the most important theater of British capital adventure in the world, and perhaps not surprisingly, the British suddenly took a keener interest in the area.

On top of that, the Germans established a colony along the arid west coast of southern Africa, known as German South West Africa (concurrent with the future Namibia) in 1885. Suddenly, the Germans had pitched their flag in the middle of a British sphere of influence, and their intentions were quite naturally suspect. A natural ideological alliance existed between the Germans and the Boer, and this hinted at the possibility of a more formal political and military alliance being established. This would have immediately jeopardized British control of the key southern African ports, and no less importantly, British economic dominance of the diamond and gold fields.

As the great European powers were beginning to jostle ever more acrimoniously at home, and as their interests were beginning to increasingly globalize, the political dynamics of southern Africa began to seem progressively less tenable. War on some level was growing more inevitable by the day.

The Jameson Raid

"There is only one possible settlement – war!" - Alfred Milner

An obvious corollary of Britain's dominance over the Transvaal gold fields was a huge influx of British expatriates. The Boer, a bucolic and conservative people, lacked the technical expertise to deal with the kind of deep-level industrial mining in the Transvaal, which required large numbers of skilled workers to function. It was not only British capitalists and industrialists who financed the Transvaal mining industry, but largely British-affiliated workers who ran the mines and attended to the innumerable peripheral and support industries associated with the mines. Most of this took place in the thriving and chaotic mining city of Johannesburg, and in due course, Johannesburg became an English speaking region. For its part, the central government of the Transvaal, located in the capital city of Pretoria, levied heavy taxes against the mining industry and ran several lucrative and questionable monopolies over such vital commodities as explosives.

All of this was extremely lucrative, but at the same time, the Transvaal Boer, led by an aging patriarch named President Paul Kruger, resolutely resisted calls by various expatriate lobbies (the Boer referred to the non-Boer émigré community as Uitlanders, or Foreigners) to provide limits on taxation, and representation commensurate with that taxation. The Uitlander population, by the latter half of the 19th century, had grown in numbers and capital influence to such a degree that a free grant of voting rights would have meant, in practical terms, an Uitlander government in the Transvaal. Gone in an instant would be the cherished Boer ideal of independence, sovereignty, and freedom from British domination. Kruger could simply not countenance this.

Kruger

It would be impossible to overstate the degree of mistrust and antipathy felt by the Boer towards the British. British imperialism at the close of the 19th century was a vast, global phenomenon, more powerful and wide-reaching in every regard than even its closest European competitors. It therefore stood to reason that two malingering republics, located on a continent dominated by European imperial powers, existed under the constant threat of absorption. The Boer leadership, in turn, burned with paranoia, and they were constantly vigilant to any possible hint of a British plot, direct or indirect, real or imagined, to gain control over the republics, the Transvaal Republic in particular.

It was into this political backdrop that Cecil John Rhodes entered in 1870. Rhodes, an unhealthy youth of limited prospects, went on to make his fortune in the diamond fields of Kimberley, a fortune that he then magnified on the gold fields of the Transvaal. Rhodes was an imperialist at heart, and he held firm to the common belief of the age that the English speaking races enjoyed a particular, God-given destiny to rule and govern the world. In his worldview, Africa, and South Africa in particular, would never reach its full potential until it had been amalgamated in its entirety under British rule. The practicalities of this vision, however, were limited, and Rhodes knew this, so he was willing to settle for as much of Africa as could be reasonably claimed on behalf of the British. Ultimately, his African imperial fiefdom would run from the southern boundaries of the Congo to the Limpopo River, but despite his best efforts, the successful unification of South Africa eluded his best efforts.

Rhodes

Politically, Rhodes occupied the office of Prime Minister of the Cape Colony, and with vast wealth at his disposal, he was in a position of enormous local power. Sometime during 1895, he formed a covert alliance with the Conservative British Colonial Secretary, Joseph Chamberlain, who happened to share his vision for a united South Africa, albeit for different reasons. Rhodes was a capitalist and a visionary, and there was always a strong strain of ideology that ran through his thinking. Chamberlain, on the other hand, was a political strategist, and he was concerned with the proximity of the Germans, the potential of a German/Boer alliance, and the likely implications this had on Britain's strategic position in Africa. Chamberlain also worried about a wider European war being inevitable.

Chamberlain

While carefully camouflaging his involvement, Chamberlain tacitly supported the development of a plot in South Africa, devised by Rhodes and supported by Rhodes' local network. In essence, the plot involved leveraging Uitlander discontent in the Transvaal to create a coup d'état. Rhodes would provide the arms and the money, and he would orchestrate the start of the coup. That trigger would take the form of a mounted force of some 600 men, drawn from the colonial militia of his territory of Rhodesia. At a predetermined time, the Uitlanders in Johannesburg would rise in rebellion, and the armed force, led by a man named Leander Starr Jameson, would ride into the city, take control of the gold mines, and then engineer the collapse of the Transvaal government.

Jameson

As it turned out, Rhodes made one major miscalculation, and it was simply that wealthy men are seldom predisposed to revolution. A great deal of hue and cry was generated, and a rather amateurish organization of the plot ensured that the Boers were well-informed of every detail, so that when the raid was launched on New Year's Eve of 1896, the Uitlanders manifestly declined to place themselves in harm's way and the raiders were met by a fully armed Boer reception party.

As Julius Caesar once remarked, if one must break the law, then do so to seize power, but in all other cases, obey it. Rhodes failed to seize power, so he simply broke the law. Chamberlain, the complicit British Colonial Secretary naturally distanced himself from the planning and denied all knowledge, leaving Rhodes to bear the consequences alone. The raiders were extradited to Britain to face trial, while Rhodes was eventually removed from all of his major business interests and forced to resign as Prime Minister of the Cape Colony. He never achieved the same level of power and influence again.

An 1896 depiction of the arrest of Jameson

Although it was an abject failure, the Jameson Raid set in motion a chain of events that would lead to war. The Uitlander crisis continued to ferment, and the British authorities in South Africa, supported by Whitehall, initiated negotiations with the government of the Transvaal over the question of Uitlander rights and liberties in the republic. These negotiations were somewhat disingenuous since the British were looking to instigate some sort of conflict, and in due course, as he was backed into a corner, President Kruger issued an ultimatum for the removal of British troops from the borders of the republic. The British press bellowed with derisive mirth at the audacity of it, as did the Victorian public, and the ultimatum was ignored.

Thus, on October 11, 1899, war was declared.

Three Sieges

"I have done my utmost for peace, despite England pushing the Boers out of their inheritance bit by bit, and taking advantage of us in every conference and native war. My hope till the present war had been for a South African Confederacy under English protection – the Cape, Natal, Free State and Transvaal all having equal rights and local self-government." – General Piet Joubert

On the eve of the war, the British armed presence in South Africa was extremely limited. The Boer, on the other hand, had been covertly arming and organizing for some time. As a result, by the time the war started, it was estimated by British intelligence that some 32,000 fighting men were on call in the Transvaal alone. These were supported by a modern and well equipped artillery division, the Staats Artillerie, an extremely functional police force, the Zuid-Afrikaansche Republiek Politie (ZARP), and a widespread and effective intelligence network. As Chamberlain had suspected, the Germans were sympathetic to the Boer, and almost all of the Boer war materiel and equipment were sourced from Germany. This cooperation fell short of a formal alliance, but Boer fighters were nonetheless armed with the latest Mauser Model 93/95 rifles, and plenty of Boer artillery had been manufactured by the Germans.

The Boer military structure was based on a commando system that had evolved as a civil defense in response to generations of frontier and border wars with black South African tribes. A permanent official within the community, known as a Veldkornet, dealt with what formal organization there was, and he both commanded and summoned the commandos when they were needed. Boer commandos, therefore, comprised an informal mounted infantry, usually highly mobile, and they embraced community-based units that consisted of all able-bodied men, urban and rural, within any given area. These men were expected to serve at a moment's notice if the call came.

The weakness in this arrangement was command. As with all informal militias, volunteers could be led but never driven. Command was based not on a rigid hierarchy, as was the case with the British Army, but by the consent of the majority, so tactics and strategy were agreed to by consensus, which inevitably resulted in a weak and variable chain of command.

At the outbreak of war, command of Boer forces resided in the hands of a 68 year old patriarch by the name of Piet Joubert, whose military experience was informal and whose command style was cautious. His combat history had been mainly during the "Kaffir Wars," the wars of pacification fought against native tribes. There certainly were younger men within the command structure, and many with more progressive ideas, but it was the elders who tended to hold sway within the military council. Consequently, the immediate strategy that evolved was cautious and conservative.

Joubert

Cautious ideology or not, the military situation at the onset very much favored the Boer. The British could rely on just a small garrison of a few thousand imperial troops and a collection of regionally organized colonial militias. The younger men within the Boer leadership, among them a brilliant young lawyer by the name of Jan Christiaan Smuts (then the Transvaal state attorney) and a charismatic farmer by the name of Louis Botha, both urged a rapid seizure of the key ports in order to prevent the landing of a British expeditionary force, which would inevitably occur at some point. This was undoubtedly a logical strategy, and had it been followed, it is possible that what many saw as an inevitable Boer defeat might have been avoided.

Smuts

Smuts and Boer guerrillas in 1901

Botha

At the same time, there were many within the higher echelons of Boer leadership, most notably Jan Smuts, who did not see much hope of an ultimate military victory for the Boer. The integration of the Boer republics into the British network of overseas territories was in some respects inevitable, and the overwhelming power of the British Empire somewhat precluded any hope of the British truly being defeated. What Smuts and others saw as more likely was a situation where war, in the Clausewitzian sense of the word, would be deployed as an instrument of politics. It was a question of under what terms and conditions the republics would submit to British superintendentship, and what could be decided by war.

Others, of course, did not see the situation in quite so nuanced a form. Anti-British sentiment was almost a religion in the republics, and among the mid-level command, ignorance of the outside world and a general lack of strategic understanding meant that many believed it was a simple question of victory or defeat.

From the beginning, the British moved wisely. The Jameson Raid had originated from the British protectorate of Bechuanaland, the modern day Botswana, and the British gambled that a build-up of forces in the same region would play on Boer paranoia, resulting in a deployment of forces away from the main strategic ports in the Cape and in Natal. The British strategy was to draw Boer forces into the north and northeast of the Transvaal, and from there the British would defend two key settlements, the diamond mining town of Kimberley and the railway depot of Mafeking. This would draw the Boer into pointless sieges that would divert and engage a disproportional amount of Boer manpower, and so long as the sieges were maintained, that manpower would be diverted away from more potentially productive targets.

When war broke out, this is precisely what happened, and the sieges of Kimberley and Mafeking began by mid-October. However, on October 12, a day after the declaration, 21,000 Boer horsemen also surged out of the Transvaal and the Orange Free State into Natal, where they laid siege to the British garrison town of Ladysmith, which most analysts agree was the signature Boer strategic blunder of the war. Without a doubt, had that force bypassed Ladysmith and thereby isolated the garrison by simply sealing road and rail access, it could have concentrated its main effort on the port town of Durban, Natal. That would have made British landings far more difficult. At the same time, had the temptation to lay siege to Mafeking and Kimberly been resisted, and the men and artillery so preoccupied been directed to Cape Town and Port Elizabeth, the Cape might also have been secured.

A picture of Boer troops in a trench outside Mafeking

The sieges of Kimberley and Mafeking were for the most part static, while Ladysmith, the more famous of the three, was much more dynamic.

The commander of British troops in South Africa was Sir Redvers Buller, a veteran of the subcontinent and many other African colonial conflicts. When the war started, Buller was dispatched from England, and he arrived in South Africa to assume his command at the end of October 1899. By then, a mixed force of some 15,000 British troops, the Natal Field Force, had been diverted to Natal from various locations and had landed under the command of Lieutenant General Sir George White. In the expectation of a Boer movement against the Natal ports, White had been advised not to deploy his troops too far inland, but upon taking command, he discovered that his immediate subordinate, General Sir Penn Symons, had already pushed advance units to two points in the Natal interior. The first of these was the garrison town of Ladysmith, located 60 miles inland of Durban, and the second was the coal mining town of Dundee, a further 25 miles northeast of Ladysmith.

Buller and his wife

White

Surrounded by hills, Dundee became the site of the first major action of the war.[1] The *Battle of Talana Hill* took place on October 20, 1899, as Boer forces occupied a prominent hill overlooking the town, and opened the action with a largely ineffectual artillery barrage aimed at the British camp. The character of the British response was direct, with a full frontal infantry advance covered by reasonably accurate artillery fire advancing directly against Boer positions. It was a punishing advance for the British, who paid dearly for their first victory, losing some 446 men in the action, including General Sir Penn Symons himself who received a fatal rifle shot in the stomach.

As advance British troops closed in on the summit of the hill, the Boer simply mounted their horses and galloped away, regrouping at a point called Elandslaagte. This cut off the British retreat to the main force in Ladysmith, which would prove to be the pattern in many of the preliminary battles that followed.

The opening stages of the war were conventional, insofar as the Boer moved in large formations, utilizing supply columns and artillery. Even still, they were significantly more mobile than the British. British columns were monolithic, and their tactical maneuvers were ponderous and predictable. In this regard, the Boers enjoyed an initial advantage.

Meanwhile, a second action was fought soon afterwards as the British attacked Boer positions at Elandslaagte to clear the lines. In what came to be known as the Battle of Elandslaagte, the

---

[1] The *Battle of Kraaipan* in the Northern Cape occurred a week earlier, which was a smaller action, and which preceded the Siege of Mafeking

British, commanded by Major General John French, scattered the Boer. General White, assessing the situation from his command room in Ladysmith, was convinced that a much larger concentration of Boer was massing to hit the advanced column, so he ordered a rapid retreat. Given that the British won a tactical victory at Elandslaagte, this had about it the flavor of an overly hasty retreat, and it immediately squandered any advantage gained. As the column entered the precincts of Ladysmith a few days later, the Boer simply closed in behind them, and positioning their siege guns on the surrounding high ground, they began to lay down a carpet of fire.

General White, in a rather ill-conceived response, sent out a strong foot and mounted force under orders to take the Boer artillery positions, but the attack was almost immediately broken against the entrenched Boer forces and an enfilade of witheringly accurate Boer musketry. This became known as the Battle of Ladysmith, and it ushered in a period of disastrous British reverses that would mark the beginning of the British counter-offensive. The British seemed to consistently underestimate the mobile fighting capabilities and the superb marksmanship of individual Boer combatants, and in long-range engagements over open ground, the advantage almost always went the Boer's way.

British soldiers at the Battle of Ladysmith

At this point in the conflict, Boer morale and cohesion were very high. They were well-armed, capably led on a detachment level, and well-mounted. British troops, on the other hand, with a command element still somewhat reliant on the tactics of the last war, deployed set-piece advances over open ground, or in the face of entrenched positions that were easily targeted and cut up by a mobile and elusive enemy. The British were armed with a state-of-the-art rifle, the .303 Lee Metford, that was capable of a high degree of accuracy and a high rate of fire, but these advantages were not properly utilized. Perhaps the only real utilitarian advance that the British

Army had made since the last major war in South Africa, fought against the Zulu, was to abandon the ubiquitous redcoat, which would have been nothing less than a joy to Boer marksmen as the hapless British troopers marched in open formation across the battlefield. British troops now adopted khaki, which proved to be a far more practical uniform for the African veld, but their battlefield tactics were still slower to evolve.

It is also perhaps worth noting that the British Expeditionary Force that set sail soon afterwards, and which would eventually number upwards of 240,000 men, included numerous colonial militias and detachments from Canada, New Zealand and Australia. They joined numerous local rough-rider style commandoes, and they introduced to the tactical rulebook of the British Army an entirely new concept of warfare. As the Boer fought an increasingly mobile campaign, utilizing marksmanship and horsemanship in combination with local knowledge, these smaller imperial units responded in kind, developing many of the ground rules of future guerrilla warfare.

In the wake of the Battle of Ladysmith, the British attack column returned to Ladysmith having suffered 140 men killed, many more wounded, and some 1,000 captured. After that, the Siege of Ladysmith began.

By the time the siege closed in on Ladysmith, the sieges of Kimberley and Mafeking had been in effect for almost a month, and the stresses of siege life had already begun to tell in both places. Regular artillery bombardments and food shortages were the main problems, and as the sieges wore on, these stresses amplified. Eventually, however, siege life settled into a predictable routine on both sides, and permeable lines allowed for some back-and-forth movement of dispatches and personnel. The Siege of Mafeking, commanded by the legendary Colonel Robert Baden-Powell, was perhaps the most isolated of all, and conditions were the most spartan, but in all instances, a high degree of creativity came into play. There was plenty of daring in the periodic breaking of the sieges, and even some gentlemanly fair play in the celebration of events and holidays.

Baden-Powell

Trapped in Kimberly at the time of the siege was Cecil John Rhodes, whose mining interests were mainly in that city. Rhodes, in keeping with his nature, frequently attempted to usurp the authority of the military commander, Lieutenant Colonel Robert Kekewich, who periodically threatened Rhodes with arrest over his constant meddling. Kimberly was a large mining settlement, so numerous industrial workshops were available to improvise weapons and protections, including an armored train. On the whole, the residents of Kimberly survived the experience without too great a hardship.

Kekewich

Ladysmith, however, was where the attention of the British Empire was mostly focused. Commanding the Boer forces was the young and charismatic field commander Louis Botha. The world would hear a great deal of Louis Botha in future years, and eventually he would emerge as the first Prime Minister of the Transvaal, and then of the Union of South Africa. He would ultimately become one of the most widely respected imperial statesmen of the 20th century. For the time being, however, he was just 37 years old, but a dynamic and gifted tactical commander.

Botha had already proved himself in the field, but the real test would come when he faced the imperious and overconfident General Buller. Buller had by then landed in Cape Town, and he was busy organizing his expeditionary force, which included an army corps of three divisions. His original intention had been to march directly northwards from Cape Town to Pretoria, taking the Orange Free State Capital of Bloemfontein en route, but the sieges complicated this, so he was forced upon arrival to modify his plan. One division was therefore sent north under the command of Lieutenant General Lord Paul Methuen to relieve the garrisons at Kimberly and Mafeking, another smaller force was sent to contain any possible uprising of Boer in the Cape, and he personally led the largest detachment by sea to Port Natal, from where he would push overland towards Ladysmith.

This monumental deployment began what has since come to be known in British military lore as Black Week. The large, heavily supported British columns immediately began to run afoul of mobile Boer commandos, and from December 10-15, the British suffered several shocking defeats.

The first of these was the Battle of Stormberg, fought on December 10, where 135 British troops were killed and 600 were captured. Next came the Battle of Magersfontein on December 11, in which 14,000 British troops advanced on Kimberley and were thrown back at the cost of 120 killed and 690 wounded. The efforts to relieve Kimberley and Mafeking were failing miserably.

The lowest point of Black Week came on December 15, 1899, when Buller, leading a column of 21,000 men, came up against a smaller force of 8,000 Transvaal Boer commanded by General Botha. Buller landed in Durban on December 6, and with surprising efficiency, was very quickly on the move. News reached him en route of the defeats at Stormberg and Magersfontein, which simply added to his impatience to deal promptly with Ladysmith in order that he could turn his attention to the wider theatre. A major obstacle to be negotiated, however, was the Tugela River, flowing off the eastern slopes of the Drakensberg and entering the Indian Ocean some 70 miles north of Durban. This barred his way, and under any circumstances, it was a formidable obstacle and a superb defensive barrier for the Boer. Buller made a direct approach on the river in the direction of the small town of Colenso, located 20 miles or so south of Ladysmith. The landscape was open, with areas of high ground scattered here and there upon which Boer reconnaissance groups carefully plotted his advance. On the opposing bank, the Boers were dug in, ready to contest the crossing.

The Battle of Colenso was not only a confused and bloody action, replete with the desperate heroism so typical of British military lore – four Victoria Crosses were awarded – but it also demonstrated the same stultifying lack of tactical creativity that was a trademark feature of Victorian warfare. Ultimately, Buller's division was thwarted in its effort to cross, and it was driven back with heavy casualties. British losses ran to 143 killed, 756 wounded, and 220 captured. The battlefield consisted largely of open ground, which gave the Boer a virtually unrestricted field of fire, and notwithstanding punishing artillery duels back and forth across the river, efforts to move infantry across the river simply proved too costly. A portion of the high ground – a hill known as Hlangwane – was occupied by the Boer, and it commanded the battlefield. So long as this was held, the Boer held the advantage.

A picture of part of the battleground

The British weren't the only ones making mistakes. The Boer did not follow-up these impressive tactical victories, allowing the British to withdraw, regroup and reorganize. Over the next few weeks, Buller received steady reinforcements, and as he waited, he modified his plan. He would now move 30 miles upstream and cross the river at two points. Once he established a bridgehead, he would move his force across in order to complete the 20 miles to Ladysmith. Crucially, he intended to attack and neutralize a heavily defended Boer position on a hill known as Spion Kop, guarding the left flank of his advance. Spion Kop, at 1,410 feet, was the commanding feature of the local landscape, and with an artillery battery positioned on top, the British would effectively command the approaches to Ladysmith.

The crossing was achieved without particular difficulty, but it was during the assault on Spion Kop that things once again began to unravel. This was perhaps the most iconic battle of Buller's advance, the Battle of Spion Kop, which has been made even more famous by the fact that the Indian barrister Mohandas K. Gandhi served on the battlefield as a stretcher bearer, as a member of the Natal Indian Ambulance Corps.

Boer forces at Spion Kop

The topography of Spion Kop resembles an extended "L," with the tail facing north and the highest point at the apex. Five distinct peaks or promontories mark the summit, and the Boer held the highest. On the evening of January 23, 1900, under cover of darkness and obscured by mist, the British climbed the hill and expelled a small Boer detachment from what they assumed was the summit. However, the daylight revealed that they had only occupied the lowest of the five summits, an acre-sized plateau exposed on three sides to Boer positions on higher ground. Entrenchment was difficult because of the hard ground, and 1,000 or more British troops thus found themselves exposed on three sides to enemy fire.

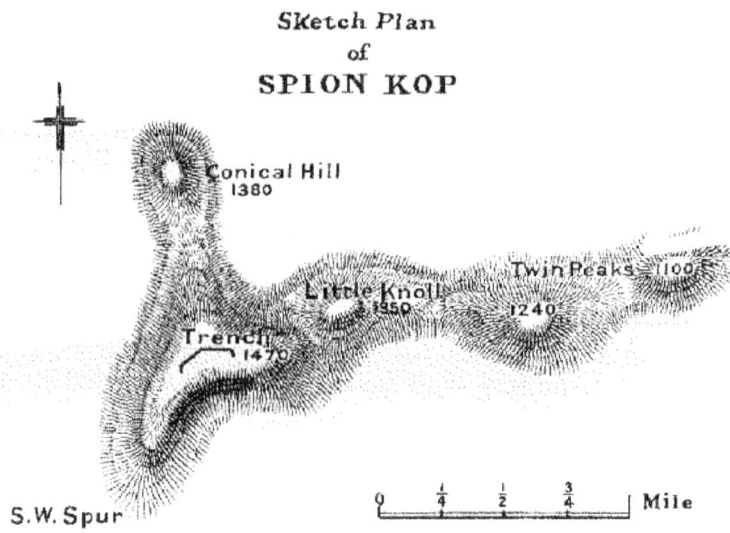

A map of the 5 peaks

Botha ordered his men to take the position before the British could move up their heavy guns. Heavy salvos of fire poured into the shallow British trenches, and casualties quickly began to mount. The Boer directed their artillery from adjacent positions, and accurate shelling added to the misery of the beleaguered British troops. Boer reinforcements then moved up and began hitting the British from the right flank. The commanding officer, Major General Edward Woodgate, was felled by a shard of shrapnel above his right eye, and his replacement, Colonel Malby Crofton, signaled the column commander, General Sir Charles Warren, by heliograph that without immediate reinforcements, all was lost. General Warren replied with the typical valor of a rear commander that the position must be held to the last. No surrender must be contemplated.

That night, the defenders held their position, absorbing dreadful casualties while tactical command gradually collapsed in the mounting chaos. Hours later, dawn rose on a scene of abject slaughter. Tormented by heat and thirst, low on ammunition, and still under withering fire, the surviving commander, Lieutenant Colonel Alexander Thorneycroft, continued to plead for permission to withdraw. In the end, in consultation with his fellow officers, Thorneycroft ordered a complete withdrawal on his own authority. "Better six good battalions safely down the hill than a bloody mop-up in the morning." He is reported to have later remarked. "I've done all I can, and I'm not going back."

A picture of dead British soldiers on the battlefield

Ironically, the Boer forces had also largely abandoned their positions, having reached their own conclusion that further defense was pointless. The fact that British defenses had also been abandoned was only accidentally discovered by two Boer Scouts, who probed the hilltop in the early afternoon and found British trenches manned only by the dead. The Boer quickly returned and hailed their victory. The British suffered 243 fatalities during the battle, most of which were buried in the trenches where they fell. Approximately 1,250 British were either wounded or captured. The Boer, on the other hand, lost just 68 men dead and 267 wounded.

Despite the setback, the sheer weight of British numbers prevailed, and Buller was able to throw a pontoon bridge across the Tugela. After that, a mass of British infantry bore down on Ladysmith, taking the last defended points of high ground along the way. The Siege of Ladysmith was lifted on February 27, 1900, having lasted for 118 days. Withstanding the siege and lifting it cost some 7,000 British casualties.

John Henry Frederick Bacon's painting depicting the lifting of the siege at Ladysmith

In time, the weight of British numbers prevailed over the sieges of Kimberly and Mafeking as well. The relief of Kimberly was achieved on February 15, 1900, and Mafeking was relieved on May 18.

Turning the Tide

"What all felt so deeply was that the fight had gone out of the Boers, that the heroes who had stood like a stone wall on the Tugela and the Modder River, who had stormed Spion Kop and Ladysmith and many other forsaken and forlorn hopes, had lost heart and hope, and gone home and forsaken their officers." – Jan Christian Smuts

Ironically, Buller would not be the commander who relieved Ladysmith, because his handling of the campaign came under considerable criticism, and he was relieved of overall command on December 23, 1899. He was replaced by General Sir Frederick Roberts, who arrived in Cape Town on January 10, 1900 with his second-in-command, General Lord Kitchener. They led an expeditionary force of some 50,000 men, supported by over 100 pieces of artillery.

The lifting of the sieges was a major psychological blow to the Boer, but perhaps even more so was an action that took place from February 18-27, known as the Battle of Paardeberg. The battle was fought along the banks of the Modder River about 20 miles east of Kimberley. At that battle, an army of 4,000 Boer, under the command of General Piet Cronjé, surrendered to the British, taking out of action 7% of the Boer forces.

Cronjé

Roberts

The series of Boer defeats that had led to the lifting of the three sieges, in conjunction with the debacle at Paardeberg, served to convince many that it would now be impossible to reasonably oppose an overwhelming British force consolidating to capture and occupy the republics. Inevitably, a defeatist mood began to creep into the ranks of the Boer commandos. These prognostications tended to be confirmed as Roberts began to rapidly advance north from the Cape to the Orange Free State, scattering Boer resistance ahead of an unopposed occupation of Bloemfontein on March 13, 1900. The tide certainly seemed to have turned. The Orange Free State was formally annexed to Britain on May 28 and renamed the Orange River Colony, after which it came under British military administration There seemed little now to hold back a lightning British advance on Pretoria.

On March 17, four days after the occupation of Bloemfontein, a meeting of the two state presidents and all of the senior commanders was held in the temporary capital of the Orange Free State, Kroonstad, located 60 miles north of Bloemfontein in the direction of Pretoria. Here it was acknowledged that attempting to counter Roberts' steamroller tactics by conventional methods was hopeless. The struggle to retain republican independence would continue, but the strategy and tactics used to achieve this would have to change. Instead of adopting a conventional defensive position to meet the British advance across a broad front, Boer forces would now be organized into smaller units, operating in a mobile configuration and no longer dependent on conspicuous supply columns. The objective would henceforth be to interdict British lines of communication, attack from the rear, and harass the British columns at every opportunity. The broad objective was simply to extend British forces, drain British resources, and eventually provoke a backlash in Britain that would lead to favorable conditions for peace.

It was agreed, therefore, that the republican forces would split up into four main commando groups. Upon the death of Joubert in March 1900, Botha had been appointed Commandant-General of Boer forces, and he would take as his sector the Eastern Transvaal, the modern day Mpumalanga Province of South Africa. Generals Christian de Wet and James Hertzog, both Free State men, would command that sector. General Christiaan Beyers would command the territories north of Pretoria, while the ageing but highly respected General Jacobus "Koos" de la Rey would take command of the western Transvaal. Second-in-command to Koos de la Rey was the 30 year old Smuts, who had until the abandonment of Pretoria served as State Attorney and was a rising star in the Boer leadership. He was a rare creature insofar as he had been born in the Cape, making him a British subject. Indeed, he had studied law at Christ's College, Cambridge, was a member of a British Bar Association, and was fully aware of British cultural and academic tradition. He was nonetheless committed to the preservation of the republics and had been a key aid to President Kruger during the tense negotiations with the British prior to the ultimatum. At the outbreak of war, he had remained in his cabinet position, but with the collapse of the government, he was naturally absorbed into the commandos at a senior rank, even though he had no prior military experience at all.

It is also important to note that the switching of tactics from conventional defensive stances to mobile offensive operations was only really possible once the older and more conservative Boer commanders had ceded authority for one reason or another to younger, more innovative men. General Christian de Wet would emerge as probably the most celebrated Boer guerrilla leader, but Botha, de la Rey, and Smuts would also go on to forge reputations as daring and innovative commanders during this period.

De Wet

Hertzog

In Pretoria, preparations began to be made to evacuate the government and prepare for an abandonment of the capital. President Kruger, 75 years old and in poor health, was put aboard a train, along with key members of his cabinet, and sent east towards Lourenço Marques, the main Portuguese East African port. Waiting for him there was the Dutch ship *Gelderland*, sent by Wilhelmina of the Netherlands to carry the Transvaal president away to safety. He would never return from his exile.

As Kruger's train steamed eastward, an enormous British expeditionary force advanced steadily on Pretoria in three parts, with two bearing up from the south commanded by General Lord Roberts himself and a third approaching from Natal under the command of Buller. By June 4, Lord Roberts had advanced to within just a few miles of the city. Johannesburg had been taken relatively easy on May 31, 1900, since it was already largely a British settled city, and after that Roberts set his sights on Pretoria. General John French, commanding the 1st Cavalry Brigade, was detached from the main force and sent west, via the small town of Krugersdorp, to circle around Pretoria and position himself to the north behind enemy lines.

This was an odd move under the circumstances. Had Roberts deployed French and his mobile force east of Pretoria instead of west, he would have been able to capture the vital Delagoa Bay railway line, upon which Kruger had recently slipped away, cutting off any further Boer retreat and blocking the obvious route of escape that the Boer defenders and leadership would take. In all likelihood, however, Roberts probably gave no consideration to the possibility that the Boer civil and military leadership would do anything other than surrender upon the occupation of Pretoria. In the British rulebook of warfare, the capture of the enemy's capital marked the end of the war, and the idea that the Boer would fall back on their time-honored principle of mobile warfare by abandoning their cities and taking to the countryside likely never occurred to him.

Behind the lines, however, de Wet had already begun mounting hit-and-run attacks against British positions, attacking from the rear, scoring several victories in quick succession, capturing quantities of arms and supplies, and inflicting significant casualties. Kitchener was promptly deployed south by Roberts to deal with this unexpected turn of events, but de Wet remained elusive. On the evening of June 12-13, Kitchener's guard unit was hit in a surprise raid, forcing Kitchener himself to flee the scene in his pajamas and take refuge in a nearby Yeomanry camp.

Kitchener

As this was going on, Roberts formally annexed the Transvaal on September 1, 1900, and satisfied that the war was effectively over, he handed over command of what he believed would be no more than extensive mopping up to his second-in-command, Lord Kitchener. He returned to England in late November to take up his new role as commander-in-chief of the British Army.

Unbeknownst to British leaders, the annexation of the two republics was premature. The British controlled the administrative centers, but the Boer held sway in the countryside. Roberts was still on the high seas heading back to England when the guerrilla war in South Africa escalated dramatically. On December 13, 1900, a Boer force commanded by de la Rey, Smuts, and Beyers surprised a British force at Nooitgedacht, west of Pretoria, and overran their camp. British losses were 109 killed, 186 wounded, and at least 368 taken prisoner, while the Boers lost only 32 killed and 46 wounded. This would form the pattern for the next few months.

In mid-December, Hertzog crossed the Orange River and entered the Cape Colony with a large force, intending to take the fight directly to the British in hopes of provoking a large-scale Boer rebellion in the Cape. In fact, the Cape Dutch had not and would not actively enter the war in big numbers. Some did on an individual basis, maybe 5,000 in total, but Hertzog's invasion did at least relieve the pressure elsewhere. Guerrilla activities elsewhere continued, with the western Transvaal, under de la Rey and Smuts, becoming arguably the most active region.

While they ramped up the guerrilla tactics, the Boer launched a parallel diplomatic offensive. The British, never popular in Europe, attempted to portray the ongoing action as the mopping up of limited resistance, while the Boer sought to counter this by assuring the international community, including the Americans, that they were still very much engaged in the struggle. Boer officials were sent to various European capitals and the United States in an effort to secure arbitration and support for a continuation of the struggle. However, while there was a great deal of expressed sympathy for the Boer's position, very little support or practical aid came about as a result of these efforts.

Perhaps one of the most noteworthy actions of the guerrilla phase of the war was General Smuts' invasion of the Cape Colony, which began early in September 1901 and followed up on Hertzog's unspectacular effort. This was undertaken for the same basic reason, but it proved much more successful, cementing Smuts' reputation as a gifted military commander and setting him on the path to attain one of the highest military offices in the British Empire.

Although the greater strategic objective of this ambitious raid was never achieved – the Cape Dutch still stayed out of the war – the episode was a remarkable tactical success insofar as some 350 mounted men successfully remained at large in the colony until the war was eventually concluded with a treaty. Although hounded relentlessly by British and loyal columns, it succeeded in remaining operational, raising its force to an eventual 4,000, and at times getting within 150 miles of Cape Town itself.

The British Response

"I fear there is little doubt the war will now go on for considerable time unless stronger measures are taken ... Under the circumstances I strongly urge sending away wives and families and settling them somewhere else. Some such unexpected measure on our part is in my opinion essential to bring war to a rapid end." – Lord Kitchener

It soon became clear to Kitchener that he had been left with a job far greater than simply mopping up. A relatively small, mobile Boer force now had the British running around in circles across the vast spaces of South Africa, with no apparent intention of surrendering. What Kitchener was essentially confronting was the same kind of battle conditions that future counterinsurgency strategists would deal with in later African wars: an asymmetric military equation whereby the enemy enjoyed intimacy with the landscape and the broad sympathy of the non-combatant population. The campaign was now as much against the Boer as the almost limitless expanses of the South African Veld. The time-honored use of mass maneuver was irrelevant, and an entirely new strategy was required.

The first consideration was Boer support and supply. Now largely estranged from formal weapons procurement, the commandos were increasingly dependent on captured weapons and supplies. For this, Kitchener introduced severe penalties, including summary execution for any Boer combatants captured wearing British Army uniforms or using British equipment and weapons. That proved to have a minor impact; since they came from a largely agrarian population, almost every Boer fighter in the field was connected to a farm or rural homestead.

Since the Boer commandos were typically deployed on or near their home districts, a movement to and from the home front and the front-line was ongoing. Kitchener, therefore, conceived very quickly the advantage of cutting off this avenue of support. In fact, Roberts had previously ordered the destruction of rebel Boer farms in the Cape quite early on during his inland advance, but this was largely punitive rather than preventative, and also perhaps for the purpose of looting livestock. He regarded such targets as legitimate since Boer farms supplied the commandos with food, fodder for their horses, information with regard to British troop movements, and medical care to the wounded. Thanks to this, Kitchener was offered a precedent for a much wider implementation of the program, which is precisely what he did.

The British scorched earth policy went into effect piecemeal, but it quickly gathered intensity, and ultimately some 30,000 Boer farms and homesteads were burned or torched, with the additional destruction of associated black homesteads. This resulted in the devastation of over 100,000 homes. Alongside this, 40 towns and villages of various sizes were razed to the ground. As a consequence, large areas of the Orange Free State and the Transvaal were laid to waste.

In conjunction with this, Kitchener authorized the use of internment camps to further isolate Boer fighters from their families, which would hopefully have the added effect of undermining the will to fight on the part of those whose families were now suffering the punitive effects of the war. The term "concentration camp" has fallen into disfavor in recent years for obvious reasons, and historians tend to prefer "internment camps" when describing the British camps, but the lingering effects of this experience still reside very much in the collective consciousness of the South African Afrikaans community.

A camp near Cape Town

The first two camps, situated in Pretoria and Bloemfontein, started as authentic refugee camps housing those displaced by the war for one reason or another, or for the families of Boer commando members who had surrendered. But once the scorched earth policy was rolled out, the families of active commando members were also driven into these camps, at which point they acquired the name "concentration camps."

It is also worth noting that a large number of blacks associated with Boer farms and homesteads were likewise interned under similarly restrictive conditions, but in separately located camps. Black families, whether or not they were actually associated with Boer families, were as deeply affected by the scorched earth policy as the other rural inhabitants of the Orange Free State and the Transvaal. According to some accounts, there was an ulterior motive on the part of the British in targeting black civilians in this manner, and this was to gain a source of captive or coerced labor for the various noncombatant roles necessary to support such a vast British expeditionary force. These roles not only included such necessary functions as wagon drivers, stockmen, herders and general camp labor, but also more specialized roles such as tracking and reconnaissance, for which they were often ideally suited. The British made widespread use of them, as did the Boer, albeit to a lesser degree.

After awhile, the use of camps, the scorched earth policy, and the extreme social hardships that all of this imposed upon the civilian population began to attract the attention of British liberals and humanitarians. A broadly conservative government was in power in Britain at the time, and the South African situation, now widely considered a social blight, provided the opposition Liberal party with partisan political ammunition. This was aided considerably by the work of one of the first and most influential British humanitarians and philanthropists of the age, a formidable woman by the name of Emily Hobhouse, who almost singlehandedly exposed and publicized the South African concentration camps.

Hobhouse

The British authorities in South Africa pursued a multi-tier system in the camps, insofar as ration distribution and general comforts within the wires were made available to a greater degree to the families of those men who voluntarily surrendered. Resources were withheld from the families of those men who did not. The result was widespread hunger and disease within the camps, and figures later produced suggest that some 4,177 women died, 22,074 children under the age of 16 died, and 1,676 non-combatant men died. It's estimated that the population in the camps numbered 85,000-94,000.

On June 18, 1901, Hobhouse produced a report following a tour of inspection of many such camps, entitled *To the S.A. Distress Fund, Report of a visit to the camps of women and children in the Cape and Orange River Colonies*. The damning nature of this report not only provoked measured concern in Parliament but also widespread revulsion among the wider Victorian British public, further consolidating a growing anti-war movement. There were many within the British establishment who began to ask whether the annihilation of the Boer and the absolute destruction of their lives and livelihoods could be considered a legitimate tactic of war.

Naturally, Kitchener came under increasing criticism, and his antipathy towards Emily Hobhouse caused him often to refer to her as "That Bloody Woman," a moniker that she apparently accepted with a great deal of pride and self-satisfaction.

In the meanwhile, she continued her public campaign, publishing and lecturing widely and collecting funds to improve conditions in the camps. To Lord Kitchener, she wrote, "I hope in future you will exercise greater width of judgement in the exercise of your high office. To carry out orders such as these is a degradation both to the office and the manhood of your soldiers. I feel ashamed to own you as a fellow-countryman."

In time, the British government was accused by both its opposition and members of its own party of pursuing a policy of extermination, and soon enough the question of human rights violations in South Africa became the opposition's clarion call. "When is a war not a war?" asked the Liberal Opposition Leader, Henry Campbell-Bannerman, to which he also answered, "When it is carried on by methods of barbarism in South Africa."

Against a backdrop of the explosive contents of Emily Hobhouse's report and the steady trickle of defamatory facts, the government found itself in a position requiring a response. This response took the form of a commission of inquiry, the Fawcett Commission. The Fawcett Commission was headed by a woman, Millicent Fawcett, a leader of the woman's suffrage movement who led an all-woman panel, making it quite unique for the time. Fawcett was a Liberal-Unionist, nominally a government insider, and the administration hoped for leniency in her report, but that was not to be the case. Fawcett submitted a report that went even further than Hobhouse in its unrestrained criticism of Kitchener's methods. As a result, responsibility for the administration of the camps was handed over to the civilian authorities, philanthropic organizations were given access, and conditions steadily began to improve.

Fawcett

It was broadly concluded that Kitchener had not pursued a deliberate policy of extermination, but simply that the scale of camp administration, and the level of priority the camps occupied in the overall military equation, inevitably resulted in unacceptable neglect. Kitchener was a soldier, not a civilian administrator, and the deployment and use of a system of camps to accommodate those who were accumulated there as a byproduct of a unique war was simply too new.

Other commentators and subsequent historians have been less charitable. Kitchener, they argue, used the deplorable conditions and the suffering of the inmates as propaganda. Word of what was taking place would inevitably leak to the front lines, and naturally, it would add incentive to many Boer men sitting on the fence to surrender. When no longer able to practically do this, Kitchener changed tack, ordering that his forces in the field not bring in women and children for internment but send them across the lines to join the fighting men. Thus encumbered, the commandos would find it increasingly difficult to survive, let alone maneuver, and once more, surrenders would be encouraged.

On the battlefield, Kitchener was no less diligent in applying his revised military policy. Roberts had begun a program of fortifying strategic bridges, railway junctions, and other places of importance against Boer attacks, and Kitchener began to expand on this program with the construction of blockhouses. These were in essence strong-points located in a grid system across the great expanses, linked by barbed wire. They eventually numbered 8,000 and were manned by a garrison of 60,000 soldiers and supported by 25,000 non-white auxiliaries. The blockhouse system was probably only useful in combination with the mass drives that Kitchener also implemented, but as an obstruction to free Boer movement across the landscape, they were certainly of at least some value. The drives were mass infantry movements mounted to keep the Boer mobile, and where possible to trap them against blockhouses and large garrison forces. This was feasible in the open country of the Orange Free State, and although some success was recorded, on the whole, against the mobility of the Boer commandos, it was not all that impactful. To patrol railway lines, which were always vulnerable, armored trains were deployed, but again, they were too few and too cumbersome to really have any widespread effect.

While no one policy was terribly successful on its own, all of these policies succeeded in wearing down Boer resistance, and by the beginning of 1902, a combination of dwindling numbers, hunger, diminishing supplies, and a general sense of hopelessness had begun to erode Boer morale. By April 1902, there were approximately 21,000 Boer combatants left active in the field, many without horses, rifles, or ammunition. British forces in South Africa numbered 240,000 at the peak of deployment, with huge numbers of auxiliaries. It was beginning to become clear to Boer leadership that the struggle could not continue for much longer, and at the very least, some kind of a negotiated peace would be preferable to their annihilation.

The Peace

"History writes the word 'Reconciliation' over all her quarrels." – Jan Christiaan Smuts

By April 1902, Kitchener was at his wit's end over the entire conflict, and he was anxious to see it end. Under safe conduct, he allowed the Boer leadership to meet in the town of Klerksdorp on the border of the Transvaal and the Orange River Colony. Attending this meeting, among others, were Transvaal President Schalk Burger, Transvaal military commander Botha, General Koos de la Rey, and Orange Free State President Martinus Steyn. General de Wet and General Hertzog were also in attendance. The Transvaalers tended to be more open to considering peace negotiations, while the Orange Free Staters, on the whole, took a more trenchant position, arguing for a continuation of the war. A more pragmatic presence was General Smuts, who, although not ranked among the top tier of Boer leadership, was present because of his legal training and his clear understanding of British diplomatic process.

Prominent on the British side was Alfred Milner, an extremely influential character in British South Africa and one of the original architects of the war. By 1902, the geopolitical balance was moving towards a confrontation of some sort between the two major power blocs of Europe, and Milner was looking at the world in this context. The British Empire had reached the apex of its geographic scope, and the question was now less one of continued global expansion than the consolidation of the British Empire into a form that would not only accommodate the growing mood of independence among such overseas dominions as Canada, Australia, New Zealand and India, but one that would maintain such cohesion in the face of widespread war. South Africa was the only substantive British overseas territory that was home to a white European population that did not identify fundamentally as British. The smaller African territories, and such similar territories elsewhere, were British colonies and not British dominions, and their native populations did not at that point warrant consideration as independent entities. The Boer could not be classified that way.

Milner

These considerations compelled Milner to seek a permanent British dominance in South Africa, in order that South Africa as a future British dominion would stand alongside the other major pillars of the empire when push came to shove. In part, his strategy to achieve this was to encourage the inflow of British capital for reconstruction, the mass immigration of British labor to facilitate industry and mining, and the imposition of the English language as the language of government, the judiciary, and education. In the face of all of this, the petty anxieties of a minor race seeking to preserve their identity counted as very little.

Thus, when the Boer committee returned its position on peace, marking as its minimum negotiating position the retention of independent Boer rule over the republics, Milner dismissed this outright. Unconditional surrender was his minimum negotiating position, and he would not be moved.

Kitchener now had to become something of a diplomat. He took aside the more moderate Boer leaders, like Botha and Smuts, and expressed his opinion that under the current conservative establishment in Britain, concessions of that magnitude would be impossible. A brutal and costly war had been fought and funded by the British for the purpose of adding South Africa to the British sphere of influence, and that, at the very least, was what was expected. However, he reminded the Boer that an election in Britain was imminent, and the likelihood would be that a Liberal government would follow. Given the Liberal position over such issues as the internment camps and other harsh realities of the war, the Boer should wait for the elections to begin sounding the British government out for a more equitable distribution of power and resource.

Smuts, of course, recognized this immediately. His history, his training, and his past engagement with the British softened his view, and naturally, he was better placed than his more bucolic comrades to recognize that the independence of a small race in a larger, imperial world was temporarily impractical. He did not like it, but he realized that it was unavoidable, at least in the short term. On his side stood Botha, now a very influential figure among the Boer, and it was with this fundamental realization that the two men guided the Boer establishment on the next step towards a negotiated peace.

On May 15, 1902, a grand council of Boer leaders gathered under an expansive marquee in the market town of Vereeniging, 40 miles southeast of Johannesburg, and here the final Boer position would be established. A series of difficult and acrimonious discussions took place, with moderates led by Smuts and Botha grappling against hardliners led by de Wet and Hertzog. There remained a strong Boer army in the field, and the war could easily be continued for a season or two, as the hardliners pointed out, but what, ultimately, would be the result of this? Terms of surrender could, under current circumstances, be negotiated that would salvage the Boer language, customs and national ideals. In the event of an unconditional surrender, all of that would be lost. Instead, the Boer would indeed be a subject people of the British crown, but they could retain their identity as a separate people and could live to fight a different kind of war on another day.[2]

---

[2] A point worth noting is that Smuts negotiated a key clause in the agreement that limited any black involvement in future government. Part of the British stated reason for entering the war was the disparity in rights available to whites, Indians and blacks in the Transvaal, and certain promises were made to grant greater inclusion to blacks and Indians upon an eventual British victory. Milner had argued that non-white voting rights would be implemented upon a grant of self-government. Smuts had altered that terminology to read that non-white voting rights would be considered upon a grant of self-government, which effectively pushed back that possibility until such time as the white minority accepted it, which in the event never occurred.

On May 17, 1902, Smuts, Botha, and Hertzog were sent to negotiate with Milner. Negotiations were rancorous and painful, but in the end, in exchange for their survival, the Boer leadership accepted the loss of their independence and an acknowledgement of British sovereignty over the republics. At the same time, extremely generous reconstruction funding was authorized, which Milner distributed quickly, dramatically easing the conditions of a great many impoverished Boer.

Moreover, the treaty, known thereafter as the Treaty of Vereeniging, left open the possibility of self-government under the terms of British dominion. This provision was vague, and its terms were unspecified, but it held promise for the future, and for the time being, that was enough.

Amanda Calitz's picture of the table on which the treaty was signed

The events that followed the Boer War and the treaty quickly brought about the creation of modern South Africa. The two new colonies of the Orange River and the Transvaal were incorporated into the British Empire, under military rule initially and then under formal British administration, with Milner serving as de facto governor-general of South Africa. He implemented his policy of promoting British capital and immigration vigorously, with mixed results.

Initially, the old Boer leadership, with Botha and Smuts now somewhat leading the pack, retreated into the background and refused any kind of engagement with the colonial government on any level. Milner did try to draw prominent Boer leaders into the various new colonial administrations, but this was almost always unsuccessful. No Boer leader would formally associate with the British government, which left Milner entirely accountable for the results of his policies.

Milner was confronted by the need to restart the Transvaal mining industry in order to jumpstart the economy. British capital was available to achieve this, but British labor was slow to avail itself of the opportunity. Black labor at that point was not sufficiently developed to fill the gap, so Milner was forced to contemplate imported Chinese indentured labor. This proved so universally unpopular, both in South Africa and in Britain, that it brought down the British government and discredited Milner and his entire pro-British policy in South Africa.

This was precisely the moment that Kitchener had predicted, and a Liberal victory in the 1906 British general election offered the opportunity for General Smuts to open negotiations. A strong personal sympathy and friendship developed between Smuts, who was a man of towering intellect and great statesmanship, and the new British Prime Minister, Henry Campbell-Bannerman. Smuts' position was simply that Britain would be wise to cultivate the friendship of the Boer since it would be they who would ultimately decide the direction in which South Africa would tilt when the time came for taking sides in a global war. Campbell-Bannerman agreed, and the broad terms for the self-government of the colonies were established.

Campbell-Bannerman

Self-government within the British Empire implied a domestically elected legislature, prime minister, and cabinet, under the broad and very loose terms of British superintendentship. This was the status of all the substantive British overseas dominions at that time, and it was seen in South Africa as an obvious precursor to South African dominion status within the Commonwealth. An election was held in 1907, and in the Orange River Colony, Abraham Fischer became the first (and only) prime minister. In Transvaal, Botha was similarly elected, with Smuts as his deputy.

Fischer

The next constitutional development was the amalgamation of all four British territories in South Africa into a single unified colony. Again, it was Smuts who led the process, which was largely one of reconciling the various peculiarities and race policies of each colony into a single constitutional format. The Cape, for example, enjoyed a long tradition of free franchise and liberal race policies, while the Transvaal remained deeply conservative and antagonistic towards any non-white inclusion in government or the administration. The British, on the whole, were amicable to South African unity, but they were forced by circumstance and political reality to swallow an overall race policy that was extremely retrogressive when compared to contemporary British thinking.

Nonetheless, the Union of South Africa was formalized by Parliament on September 20, 1909, and it came into being on May 31, 1910. A few years later, South Africa would be playing an important role in World War I. At the outbreak of war, Britain lacked the necessary organization and manpower to deal with the occupation of German South West Africa and German East Africa, so this task was assigned to South Africa, which would have to rely on its own resources. Almost at the moment that this understanding was reached, however, a rebellion broke out in the ranks of the Union Defense Force, and a significant number of anti-British South African troops attempted to cross into German South West Africa in order to declare for the Germans. It must be remembered that Germany had been the closest thing to a foreign alliance that the old republics had ever enjoyed, and a great many Afrikaans speaking servicemen did not see the Germans as the enemy. Furthermore, they recognized an opportunity to overthrow British rule in South Africa now that the British Empire was engaged in a European war.

Ultimately, Smuts, as Minister of Defense, crushed the rebellion, and he guided South Africa into World War I as a loyal member of the British alliance. This would also be the case in World War II, but that conflict would bring about the advent of the South African republic, and the descent of South Africa into its darkest phase of statutory racism and apartheid.

Online Resources

Other titles about South Africa on Amazon

Other titles about the Boer War on Amazon

Bibliography

Berger, Carl (1970). The Sense of Power; Studies in the Ideas of Canadian Imperialism,: 1867–1914. University of Toronto Press. pp. 233–34. ISBN 978-0-8020-6113-3.

Bester, R. (1994). Boer Rifles and Carbines of the Anglo-Boer Warb. Bloemfontein: War Museum of the Boer Republics.

Blake, Albert (2010). Boereverraaier. Tafelberg. p. 46.

"Case Name: Anglo-Boer: Britain's Vietnam (1899–1902)". American University of Washington D.C Trade Environment projects. Retrieved 21 July 2016.

Desai, Ashwin; Vahed, Goolem (2015). The South African Gandhi: Stretcher-bearer of Empire. Stanford University Press.

"Miscellaneous information: Cost of the war". AngloBoerWar.com. 2015. Retrieved 12 September 2015.[unreliable source?]

Chase, Sean (4 November 2012). "Dragoons remember the heroes of Leliefontein". Daily Observer.

Daily Mail (5810). 16 November 1914. pp. 4 ff. ISSN 0307-7578. Missing or empty |title= (help)

Duffy, Michael (22 August 2009). "Sam Hughes Biography". firstworldwar.com.[unreliable source?]

Cameron, Trewhella, ed. (1986). An Illustrated History of South Africa. Johannesburg,: Jonathan Ball. p. 207.

Cartwright, A. P (1964). The Dynamite Company. Cape Town: Purnell & Sons.

Davis, Richard Harding (1900). With Both Armies In South Africa. Charles Scribner Sons. p. 34, fn. 59.

"South African War (British-South African history)". Encyclopedia Britannica. Britannica.com. 31 March 2011. Retrieved 23 July 2013.

"Caring for the soldiers health". Nash's war manual. London: Eveleigh Nash. 1914. p. 309.

Farwell, Byron (March 1976). "Taking Sides in the Boer War". American Heritage Magazine. 20 (3). ISSN 0002-8738. Archived from the original on 7 January 2009.

Ferguson, Niall (2002). Empire: The Rise and Demise of the British World Order and the Lessons for Global Power. Basic Books. p. 235.

Grundlingh, Albert (1980). "Collaborators in Boer Society". In Warwick, P. The South African War. London. pp. 258–78.

Granatstein, J.L. (2010). The Oxford Companion to Canadian Military History. Oxford University Press. ISBN 978-0-19-543088-2.

Grattan, Robert (2009). "The Entente in World War I: a case study in strategy formulation in an alliance". Journal of Management History. 15 (2): 147–58.

Gronum, M.A. (1977). Die ontplooiing van die Engelse Oorlog 1899–1900. Tafelberg.

Haydon, A.P. (1964). "South Australia's first war". Australian Historical Studies. 11 (42).

Hayes, Matthew Horace (1902). Horses on board ship: a guide to their management. London: Hurst and Blackett. pp. 213–14.

Jeffery, Keith (2000). "The Irish Soldier in the Boer War". In Gooch, John. The Boer War. London: Cass. p. 145. cites

Inglis, Brian (1974). Roger Casement. London: Coronet Books. pp. 53–55.

Jacson, M. (1908). "II". The Record of a Regiment of the Line. Hutchinson & Company. p. 88. ISBN 1-4264-9111-5.

Jones, Maurig (1996). "Blockhouses of the Boer War". Colonial Conquest, magweb. Archived from the original on 13 May 2008. Retrieved 10 May 2008.

Jones, Huw M. (October 1999). Neutrality compromised: Swaziland and the Anglo-Boer War, 1899–1902. Military History Journal. 11.

Judd, Denis; Surridge, Keith (2013). The Boer War: A History (2nd ed.). London: I. B. Tauris. ISBN 978-1780765914.excerpt and text search; a standard scholarly history

Keppel-Jones, Arthur (1983). Rhodes and Rhodesia: The White Conquest of Zimbabwe, 1884–1902. Montreal, Quebec and Kingston, Ontario: McGill-Queen's University Press. pp. 590–99. ISBN 978-0-7735-0534-6.

McElwee, William (1974). The Art of War: Waterloo to Mons. London: Purnell. pp. 223–29. ISBN 0-253-31075-X.

"Relative Value of UK£: using Economic Power in 2014 (using the share of GDP)". Five Ways to Compute the Relative Value of a UK Pound Amount, 1270 to Present. Measuringworth.com. 2015. Retrieved 12 September 2015.

Marsh, Peter T. (1994). Joseph Chamberlain: Entrepreneur in Politics. Yale University Press. pp. 482–522.

Meintjes, Johannes (1974). President Paul Kruger: A Biography (First ed.). London: Cassell. ISBN 978-0-304-29423-7.

Morris, Michael; Linnegar, John (2004). Every Step of the Way: The Journey to Freedom in South Africa. Ministry of Education. pp. 58–95. ISBN 0-7969-2061-3.

Nathan, M. (1941). Paul Kruger: His Life And Times. Durban: Knox.

O'Brien, P. (1988). The Costs and Benefits of British Imperialism 1846–1914. Past & Present.

O'Leary, Michael (29 December 1999). "Regimental Rouge – Battles of the Boer War". Regimental Rouge.

Pakenham, Thomas (1979). The Boer War. New York: Random House. ISBN 0-394-42742-4.

Peddie, John (22 August 2009). "John McCrae Biography". firstworldwar.com.

Pocock, Roger S. (1917). Horses. London: J. Murray. p. viii fn. 11. ISBN 0-665-99382-X.

Powell, Sean-Andre (2015). How Did Winston S. Churchill's Experience As A Prisoner Of War: During The Boer War Affect His Leadership Style And Career?. Pickle Partners Publishing.

Onselen, Charles van (1982). "Chapter 1:New Babylon". Studies in the Social and Economic History of the Witwatersrand, 1886–1914. London: Longman. ISBN 9780582643840.

Onselen, Charles van (October 2003). "'The Modernization of the Zuid Afrikaansche Republiek: F. E. T. Krause, J. C. Smuts, and the Struggle for the Johannesburg Public Prosecutor's Office, 1898–1899". Law and History Review. American Society for Legal History. 21 (3): 483–526. doi:10.2307/3595118.

Pakenham, Thomas (1991) [1979]. The Boer War. London: Cardinal. p. 571. ISBN 0-7474-0976-5.

Pakenham, Thomas (1991a). The Scramble for Africa. p. 573. ISBN 0-380-71999-1.

Ploeger, Jan (1985). "Burgers in Britse Diens (1902)". Scientia Militaria. 15 (1): 15–22.

Pretorius, Fransjohan (2000). "The Experience of the Bitter-Ender Boer". In Gooch, John. The Boer War: Direction, Experience and Image. London: Cass. p. 179.

Pretorius, Fransjohan (2011). "Anglo-Boer war". In Jacobs, S.: Johnson, K. Encyclopedia of South Africa.

Pulsifer, Cameron (2017). "For Queen and Country: Canadians and the South African War". Canadian War Museum. Retrieved 2 February 2017.

"The South African War 1899–1902". South African History Online. 10 November 2011. Retrieved 29 January 2017.

Searle, G.R. (2004). A new England?: peace and war, 1886–1918. Oxford University Press. pp. 269–307.

Spies, S.B. (1977). Methods of Barbarism: Roberts and Kitchener and Civilians in the Boer Republics January 1900 – May 1902. Cape Town: Human & Rousseau. p. 265.

Steele, David (2000). "Salisbury and the Soldiers". In Gooch, John. The Boer War: Direction, Experience and Image. London: Cass.

Stirling, John (17 February 2009). "Gordon Highlanders (extract)". Our Regiments in South Africa. Naval and Military Press.

Surridge, Keith (2000). "Lansdowne at the War Office". In Gooch, John. The Boer War: Direction, Experience and Image. London: Cass. p. 24.

Swardt, Eric (1998). "The JJ Potgieter Manuscript" (PDF). p. 97. Retrieved 23 August 2009.

Villiers, J.C. de (June 1984). "The Medical Aspect of the Anglo-Boer War, 1899–1902 Part ll". Military History Journal. 6 (3):[page needed].

Warwick, Peter (1983). Black People and the South African War, 1899–1902. Cambridge University Press.

Watt, S (December 1982). "Intombi Military Hospital and Cemetery". Military History Journal. Die Suid-Afrikaanse Krygshistoriese Vereniging. 5 (6).

Webb, Peter (2010). "The Silent Flag in the New Fallen Snow: Sara Jeannette Duncan and the Legacy of the South African War". Journal of Canadian Studies. University of Toronto Press. 44 (1): 75–90.

Wessels, André (2000). "Afrikaners at War". In Gooch, John. The Boer War: Direction, Experience and Image. London: Cass.

Wessels, André (2010). A Century of Postgraduate Anglo-Boer War (1899–1902) Studies: Masters' and Doctoral Studies Completed at Universities in South Africa, in English-speaking Countries and on the European Continent, 1908–2008. African Sun Media. p. 32. ISBN 978-1-920383-09-1.

Wessels, André (2011). The Anglo-Boer War 1889–1902: White Man's War, Black Man's War, Traumatic War. African Sun Media. p. 79. ISBN 978-1-920383-27-5.

Wessels, Elria (2009). "Boers positions in the Klipriviersberg". Veldslae-Anglo-Boereoorlog 1899–1902. Archived from the original on 14 February 2013.

Witton, George (2003). Scapegoats of the Empire: The True Story of Breaker Morant's Bushveldt Carbineers.[full citation needed]

Yap, Melanie; Leong Man, Dainne (1996). Colour, Confusion and Concessions: The History of the Chinese in South Africa. Hong Kong: Hong Kong University Press. p. 510. ISBN 962-209-423-6.

Free Books by Charles River Editors

We have brand new titles available for free most days of the week. To see which of our titles are currently free, click on this link.

Discounted Books by Charles River Editors

We have titles at a discount price of just 99 cents everyday. To see which of our titles are currently 99 cents, click on this link.

Printed in Great Britain
by Amazon